Compo's Way

by
Alan Hiley

Maps and additional material by John N. Merrill

ISBN 1 874754 73 X

Printed & Published by
Footprint Press Ltd.,
"From footprint to finished book."
19, Moseley Street,
Ripley,
Derbyshire.
DE5 3DA

End to End Walks Series.

**FOOTPRINT
PRESS Ltd.,
19, Moseley Street,
Ripley
Derbyshire
DE5 3DA**
Tel/Fax 01773 - 512143

View from Sierra Blanca over White Mountains

International Copyright © Alan Hiley. All rights reserved. No part of this publication may be reproduced or transmitted in any form or by any means electronic or mechanical including photocopy, recording or any information storage or retrieval system in any place, in any country without the prior written permission of the publisher or John N. Merrill.

Warning - Violation is a criminal offence. This copyright is strictly enforced worldwide by the publisher and any and all violators, no matter how slight, will be prosecuted to the furthest extent of the law.

Printed, bound, marketed and distributed by Footprint Press Ltd.

© Text - Alan Hiley 1996

© Maps and additional material by John N. Merrill

© Sketches - Maragret Peter. 1996.

First Published - November 1996

ISBN 1 874754 73 X

British Library Cataloguing-in-Publication Data. A catalogue record of this book is available from the British Library.

Typeset in Bookman - bold, italic and plain 10pt and 14pt.

Designed and typset by Suncrest Ventures Ltd.

Cover sketch and drawings by Margaret Peter. © 1996

About the Author -

Alan Hiley was born in Sheffield on 11th. November 1942. After leaving school at fifteen he started his working life as a van boy delivering bread. Then after a stint as a van driver and bus driver, he joined the Sheffield Ambulance Service in 1968. Twenty-eight years on he is still working as a Paramedic. Having been an avid walker for many years this is his first book. Alan is married with four grownup children and he now lives in Dronfield, Derbyshire.

ACKNOWLEDGEMENTS

A Popular History of Sheffield. By J. Edward Vickers.

Where Twater Runs ore T'Wier. By S. Roy Davey.

High Peak Faces and Places. By Keith Warrender.

Sheffield City Battalion. By Ralph Gibson and Paul Oldfield.

Shepherds Wheel. Sheffield City Museums Publication.

I am grateful for the lovely drawings done for me by Margaret Peter.

Contents

Page No.

Introduction and How to do it.....5
Hunter's Bar and the start 6
Endcliffe Park 8
Whitely Woods 10
Forge 12
Redmires to Stanage Edge 14
Stanage Edge.....16
The Dyke Dale Disaster.....20
Strines Inn 23
Strines to Derwent Valley 24
Derwent to Flouch 28
Flouch to Hepworth 30
Hepworth to Holmfirth 34
Log.....38
Badge Order Form 39
Amenities Guide 40
Other Books by Footprint Press Ltd.....42
Other Challenge Walks by John N. Merrill 44

INTRODUCTION and HOW TO DO IT

This book was born out of three interests, my love of walking, reading about local history, and my favourite T.V. show. So the idea was to combine the three into a walk. It is not meant to be a history book but just a mention of places along the way. I have endeavoured to stay on public footpaths and roads the whole route, and I hope given a good range of terrain from parks and wooded valleys to the high desolate moors of the Peak District.

To be comfortable the walk should be done over a period of three days, the much of the route can be found on the Ordnance Survey Map, Outdoor Leisure No.1 the Peak District Dark Peak Area. I have tried to make the route as easy to follow as possible but the map and knowing how to read it is essential. The only deviation off track would be at the end of the second day for an overnight stay at Langsett, but this is only a short walk beside the Langsett Reservoir.

Alan Hiley. 1996

Maps required in walking order -

1:25,000 Pathfinder Series Sheet No. SK28/38 - Sheffield.
1:25,000 Pathfinder Series Sheet No. SK29/39 - Sheffield (North) and Stocksbridge.
1:25,000 Outdoor Leisure Map - The Dark Peak.
1:25,000 Pathfinder Series Sheet No. (714) SE 00/10 - Holmfirth and Saddleworth Moor.

Hunter's Bar and the start.

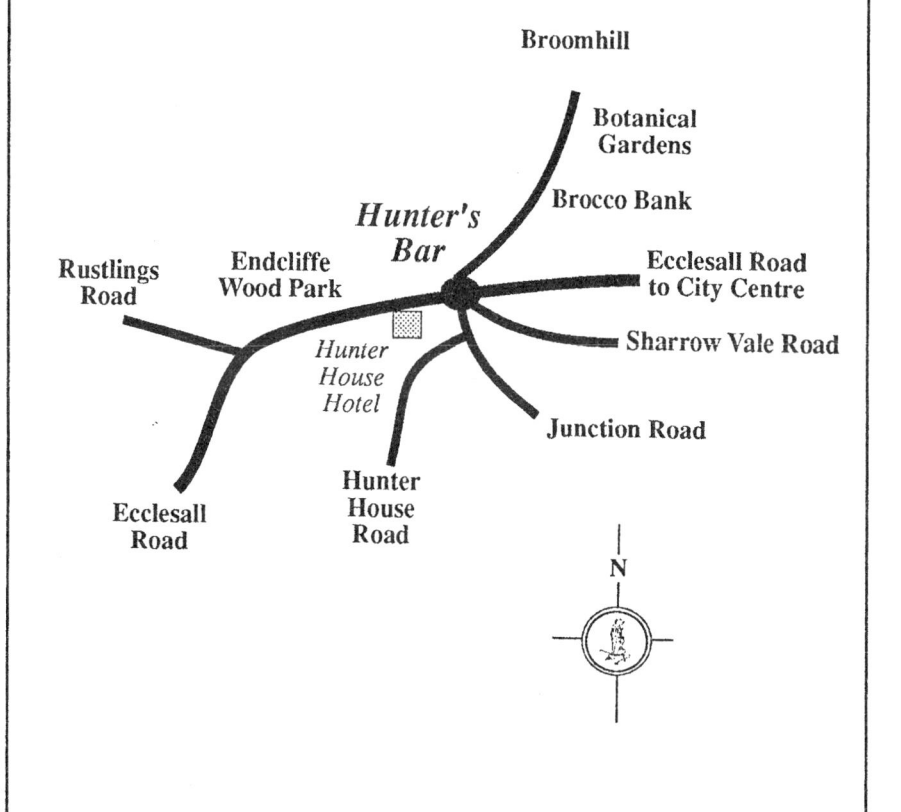

Broomhill

Botanical Gardens

Brocco Bank

Hunter's Bar

Rustlings Road

Endcliffe Wood Park

Ecclesall Road to City Centre

Sharrow Vale Road

Hunter House Hotel

Junction Road

Ecclesall Road

Hunter House Road

N

THE START - HUNTER'S BAR.

Your walk starts at the busy Hunters Bar roundabout on Ecclesall Road, The area takes it's name from the Toll Bar that stood on the old Turnpike Road at this location in the Nineteenth Century. The Bar was owned by a Mr. Hunter who lived in a large country house just above the Toll Bar. His house is still standing and now forms part of the Hunter House Hotel.

The Toll finally closed on the 31st October 1884, the last person to pass through being Mr. Haugh, a cab operator of Glossop Road, Sheffield. After he had passed through, the toll collector Mr. Speer locked his toll house and walked away now being out of a job.

A large crowd that had gathered to witness the event then took the gate and threw it into the nearby Lescar Dam.

The original gateposts with a new gate now stand proudly on the traffic island in the position they would have occupied across the old road. The Hunters Bar Toll was the last in the town to close. Whilst still at Hunters Bar I should give a mention to "Rosie", for over twenty years now she has safely seen thousands of children across this busy road, this includes my own family who used to attend the Hunters Bar School, so here's to Rosie and all the unsung heroes of the lollipop service.

Endcliffe Park - 3/4 mile.

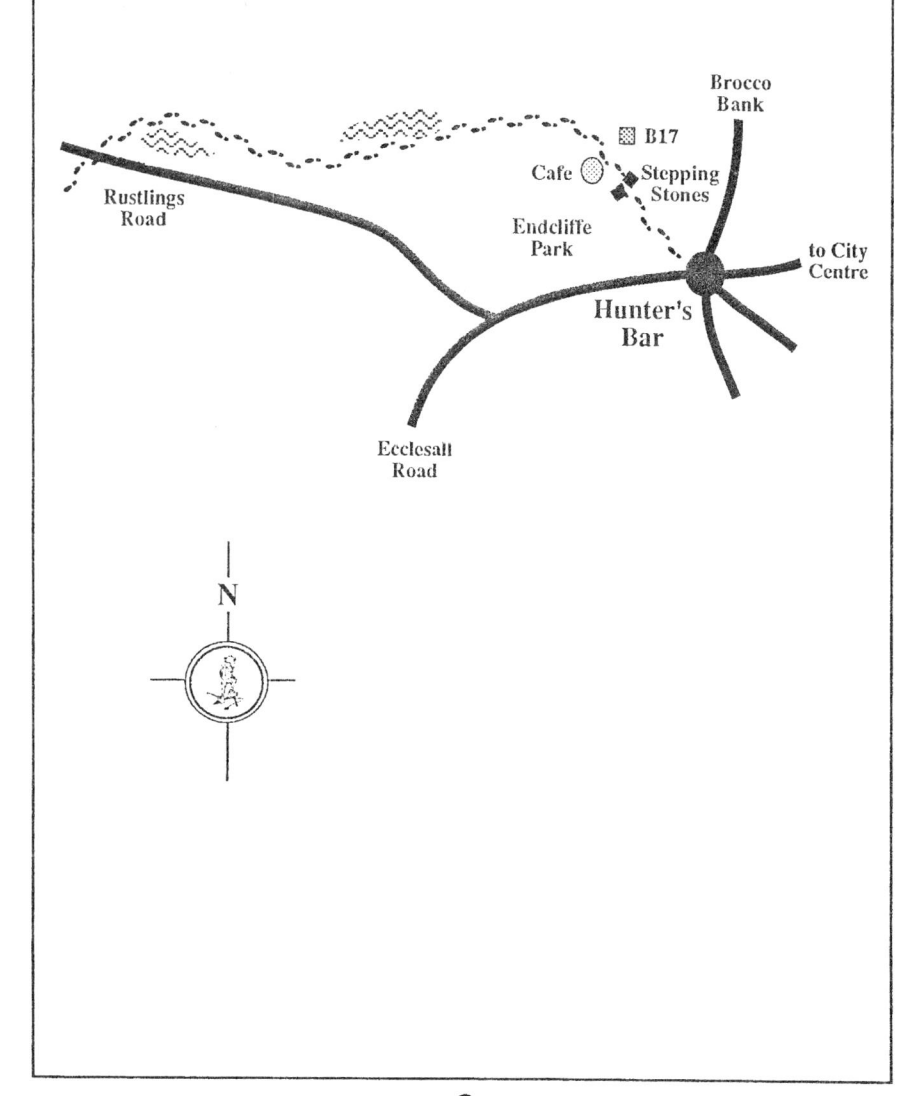

ENDCLIFFE PARK
3/4 mile.

Map -1:25,000 Pathfinder Sheet No. SK 28/38 - Sheffield.

Enter the Endcliffe Park through the gates on the roundabout, as you walk along the path you get a right royal send off by none other than Queen Victoria. The statue you see used to stand near the Town Hall in Sheffield but was moved to its present location in the 1930's. Follow the path past the children's play area, just before the cafe you will see on your right hand side some stepping stones across the River Porter. Cross the river and turn left, here you will find a large stone with a plaque fastened to it. This is a memorial to the crew of an American Airforce B17 Flying Fortress "Amigo Mio' the aircraft crashed at this spot in 1944 whilst returning from a raid over Germany. All ten crew members being killed. The Captain Lt. Krugshouser being awarded a Distinguished Flying Cross for steering the doomed aircraft away from the nearby houses. The names of all the crew are on the plaque and at the site have been planted ten American Oak trees, one for each crew member.

Continue along the path and you pass the only two remaining mill dams left in Endcliffe Park, they are now the home for many wild ducks. After leaving the second dam you leave the park and cross over the Rustlings Road and enter Whitely Woods.

B17 Memorial.

Whitely Woods
1 1/2 miles to Forge. 5 miles to Redmires

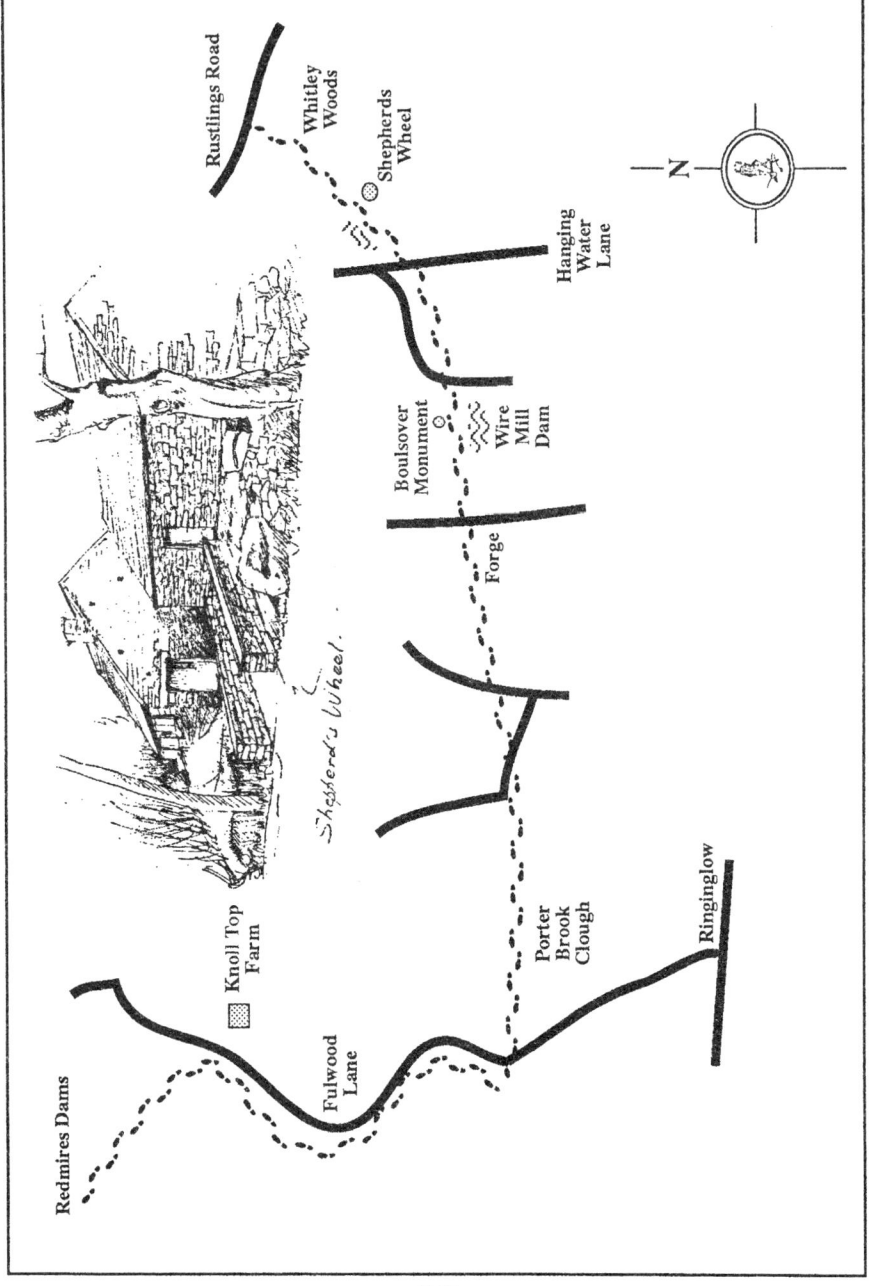

10

WHITLEY WOODS
- 1 1/2 miles to Forge
- 5 miles to Redmires.

Map - 1:25,000 Pathfinder Series Sheet No. SK28/38 - Sheffield.

As you walk along the path again on your right is an old mill dam, continue along the path and you come to the Shepherds Wheel. This is a fully restored grinding shop, the wheel dates back to the fourteenth century but takes its name from a Mr. Shepherd who rented the mill in 1794, at this time he employed ten grinders. At the other side of the river there used to be a farm but this was demolished at the turn of the century. The mill is now in the care of the City of Sheffield Museums and is open to the public with working days at certain times of the year.

Follow the side of the mill dam and you come to the sluice and goit where the water is diverted from the River. At this point cross over the road aptly named Hangingwater Road and continue along the path through the woods. Crossing over a further road follow the footpath until on your left you see some steps leading up to some old Cottages and a dam. This is the Wire Mill Dam, it is now used by model boat enthusiasts a far cry from the time the waters here turned a wheel of forty feet in diameter. In 1769 a rolling mill was installed here by Thomas Boulsover, a cutler by trade, he was the inventor of the famous Sheffield Plate. There is a memorial to this famous man by the side of the dam and one of the nearby Cottages has been named Boulsover Cottage.

Leaving Wire Mill Dam continue along the path, on your left you will see a water filled channel, this is the goit which brings the water to the dam from a quarter of a mile upstream. After a while you come to the tiny hamlet of Forge.

Boulsover Monument.

FORGE

The forge has long since gone but on your left you can still see the old Cottages the mill workers occupied. To see the area today it is hard to imagine what a hive of industry this place used to be many years ago. The lovely Cottage beside the cafe used to be a button factory, this is where Thomas Boulsover started to silver plate snuff boxes and buttons. The cafe is an ideal spot for a welcome cuppa before you continue on your way.

After leaving the cafe follow the path around the dam and follow it until you come to a lane, cross over and follow the path which forms part of the round walk. The path takes you up the lovely Porter Brook clough, at the top of the clough at the footbridge do not cross over but stay on the path to your right and up onto the road.

You have now reached the source of the river Porter on the edge of the Hallam Moors. At this point it is hard to believe that this small brook could have been the driving force for so much industry just a few miles downstream. The Porter had no fewer than Twenty Mills and dams on its six miles length before it joined the river Sheaf at Sheffield.

Turn right along the road, as you walk along you have some lovely views to your right down the Mayfield valley and Sheffield beyond. The people of Sheffield are so lucky to be surrounded by such wonderful country as can be seen from this point. It is indeed hard to believe that you are still in the boundaries of such a large City.

Continue along the lane for about a mile until on your right you come to Knoll Top Farm, take the footpath on your left opposite the bungalow. The path takes you through an old quarry, at the end of the quarry the path crosses a field to a style. At this point again a short break would not go amiss as you admire the view. If you look slightly right you will see the square clock tower at the Old Lodge Moor Hospital. Originally built in 1887 as an isolation Hospital for smallpox victims, it was built on the then Bleak Lodge Moor. I worked at this Hospital for four years when the Sheffield Ambulance service had a station there.

Forge Dam Cafe'.

One of my colleagues at that time, now retired, Terry Gorman, now paints lovely water colours of old Sheffield scenes. Alas the Hospital is now closed a victim of the health service reorganisations.

Looking directly in front you will see a large conifer plantation, this is the site of the old Redmires camp. The camp was built in 1915 to house the newly formed Sheffield City Battalion, the battalion became the (12th Service Battalion York & Lancaster Regiment).

After serving for a time in Egypt, the battalion went to France. Here they took part in the tragic battle of the Somme. On the fateful day 16th July 1916 the battalion lost 248 men killed and over 300 wounded. This appalling number of casualties marked the end of the original battalion formed in 1914. During the 1939-45 war the camp was used to house prisoners of war.

After crossing the stile turn left along the track and path which will take you down to the Redmires dams.

Redmires - Stanage Edge - 4 miles

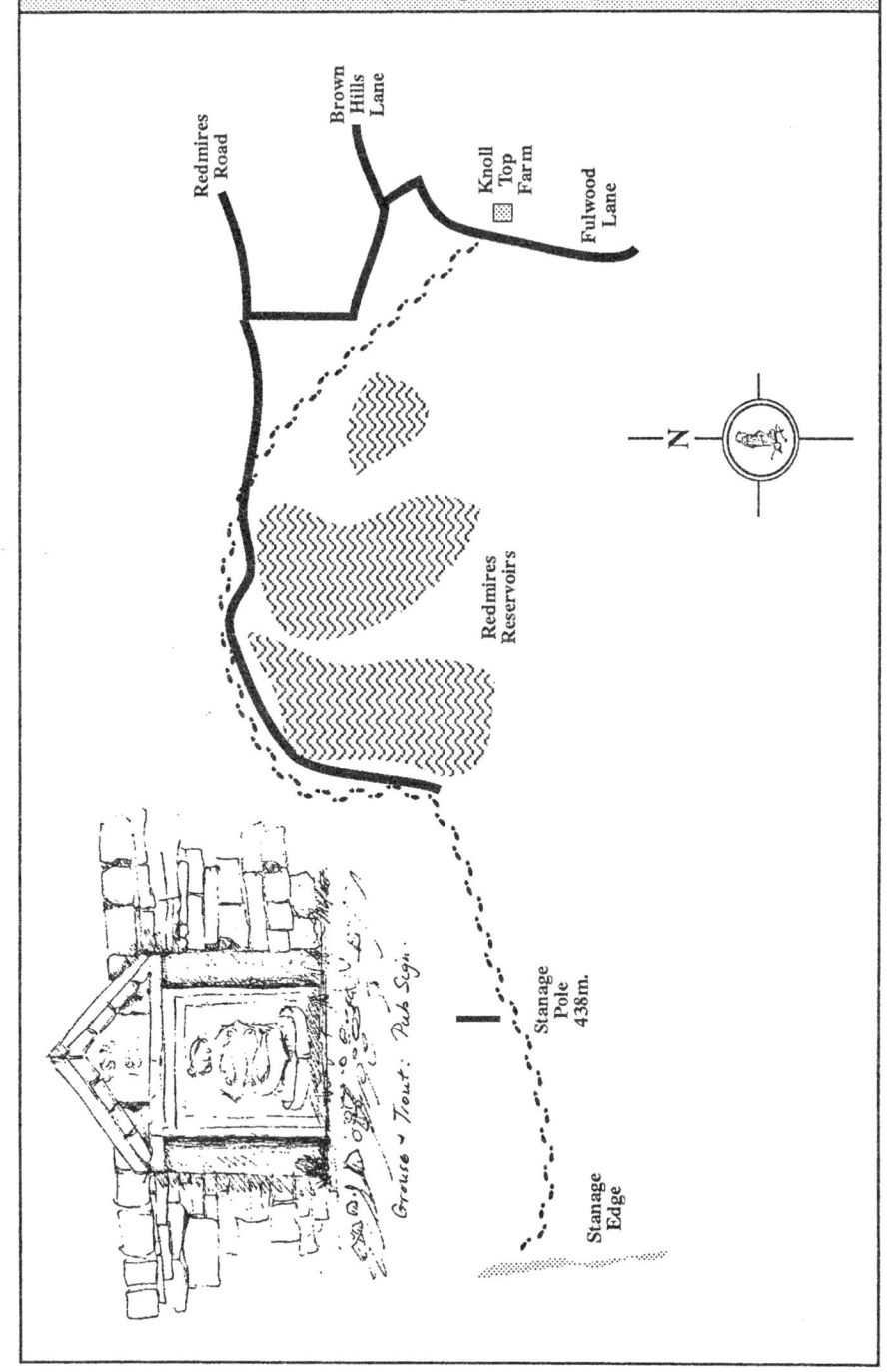

REDMIRES
to Stanage Edge - 4 miles

Map - 1:25,000 Pathfinder Series Sheet No. SK28/38 - Sheffield.

The area around the dams has been turned into a nature reserve by the Yorkshire Water Authority. The footpath takes you through the water works but is is well signposted.

As you leave the works turn left along the road, a little way along by the side of a gate you will see set into the wall a large stone with a carving of a grouse and three fish upon it. This is the old sign from an Inn which stood on this spot, it was called The Grouse and Trout Inn. During the construction of the Redmires dams it was frequented by the large number of navvies who worked at that site and had a bad reputation for the many drunken brawls which took place there. After losing its licence, in later years it became a tea shop before finally being demolished.

The dams were built in the last century to cater for the ever growing population of Sheffield, the middle dam being the first to be completed in 1836. The area is very popular with people of Sheffield and there are now picnic sites and paths for the disabled.

Follow the road around the dams until at the end you turn right up the track. This track follows the course of the old packhorse route which in turn is part of the old causeway which was the old Roman road which ran from a Settlement at Templeborough near Rotherham to another at Glossop. As you get towards the top of the track you walk on flagstones, these are thought to date from the sixteen hundreds and form part of the old packhorse road.

At the very top of the track you come to Stanage Pole, although it serves no purpose today it is the only pole left from a number of such poles that were used to guide the way across these desolate moors in bygone days. There cannot be many cities that have such a bleak and lonely place within its boundaries. As you leave Stanage Pole continue along the track down to Stanage Edge.

Stanage Edge
- 4 1/2 miles to Boots Folly.

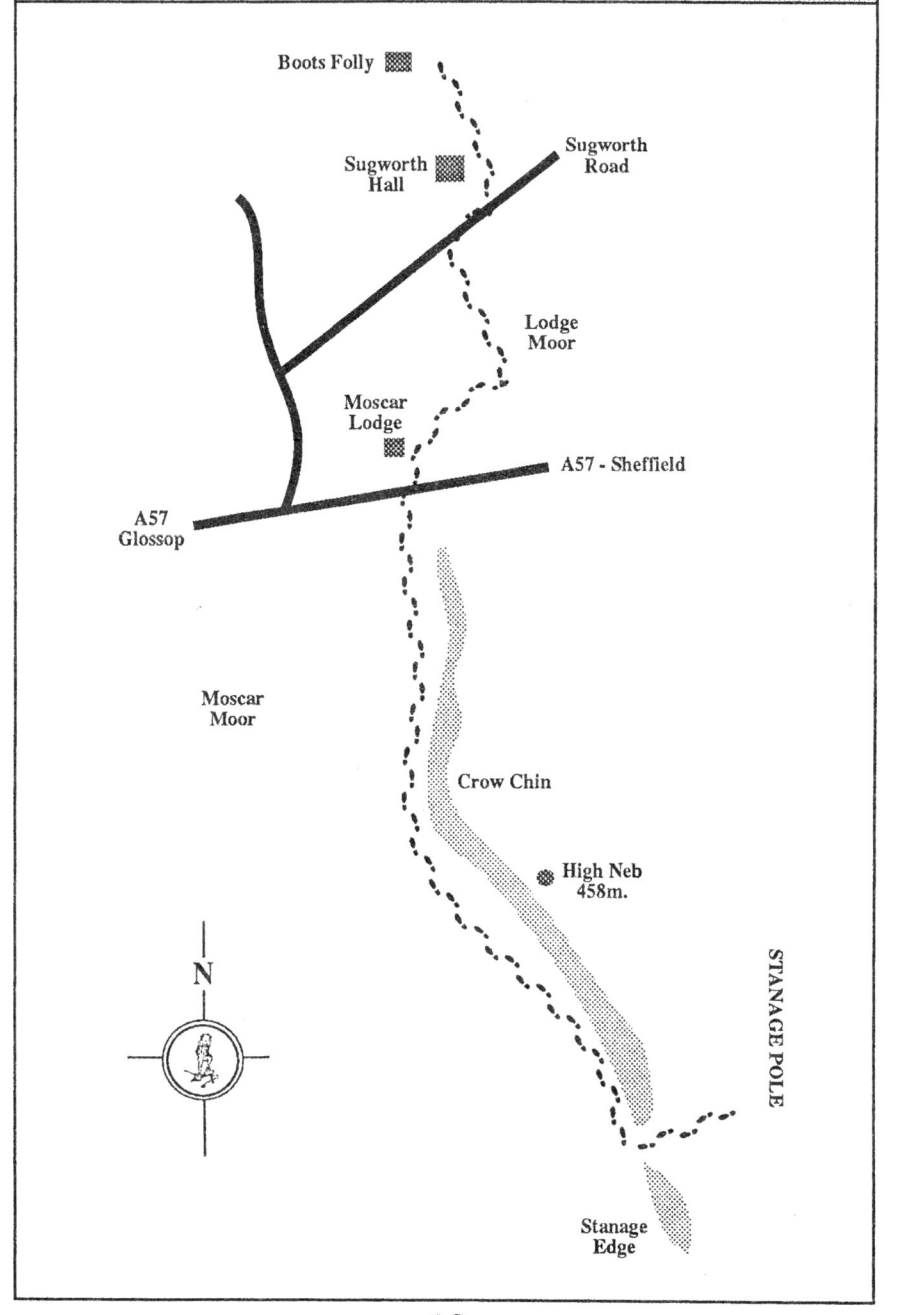

16

STANAGE EDGE
-- 4 1/2 miles to Boots Folly.

Map - 1:25,000 Pathfinder Series Sheet No. SK 29/39 - Sheffield.

As you leave the pole and walk down the track towards Stanage Edge, look over the wall to your right and you will see all alone on the open moor a lonely old house. This is the old Stanage Lodge, the house stood empty for many years but now has found a new lease of life as a clay pigeon shooting club.

Continue down the track to Stanage Edge, this is a Gritstone edge which runs for about four and a half miles in length. The edge has long been a mecca for rock climbers. At weekends at anytime of the year it is a very busy place, the views below the edge take in the Hope Valley and Hathersage. The place is also occasionally a busy place for my counterparts of the Derbyshire Ambulance Service when you get a climber taking a 'quick' way down. There is a mountain rescue post at Stanage Edge and the R.A.F. mountain rescue service also use the area for training. I myself have attended at rescues in the area during my time on the service.

Dropping down the track off the edge you come to a ladder stile over a fence on your right. Take the path over the fence and continue along with the edge on your right. As you walk along the open moors on your left are the Bamford Moors, on your right on top of the edge the trig point at High Neb is the highest point in Sheffield, at a height of 1502 ft. it makes the city of Sheffield the highest major city in Europe. a little further along the edge is Crow Chin which is the most westerly point of Sheffield. At Crow Chin are two burial mounds thought to date back 5 or 6,000 years. Stone Age tools have been found at this site.

As you continue along the path you come across a large number of old millstones, they were all hewn from the local rock, shaped but never used. One can only imagine the blood sweat and tears that went into the manufacture of these huge stones. This of course before such luxuries as fork lift trucks and mobile cranes. The only transport off the moors for these huge creations was to put an axle between three or four stones and haul them to the nearest road by horses. Indeed the path you are walking on follows the route of one of the paths down to the Manchester to Sheffield road. At this site there used to be the workshops and stables for this once busy place but there is little sign of these today.

As you walk along the path the moors on your left stretch all the way down to the Ladybower dam, this with the Derwent and Howden dams in the Derwent Valley make one of the most beautiful places in the entire Peak District. The Derwent being famous for its association with the Dambusters 617 squadron R.A.F, who used the dam to practice for their famous raid.

Millstones. Stanage

Continue along the path until you reach the main A57 Sheffield Manchester road, this road a few miles to your left becomes the notorious Snake Pass.

Crossing over the road take the path up to Moscar Lodge, as you pass the lodge at the top of the track you come to a junction of tracks, this is the old bridle road between Bradfield and Hathersage, it dates back to the 1700's.

If you look to your left by the stone wall you can see still standing a large way marker stone. At this point turn right and follow the track until you come to a footpath on your left, take this path which runs almost beside the wall until you reach a lane.

Turn right along the lane then after a short distance turn left down the drive to the lovely Sugworth Hall. A short way down the drive the path takes you to your right around the back of the hall. As you walk along the path you enter a forest of Rhododendrons, after a short walk you come to an old kissing gate. Take the path across the fields and on your left you come to an old tower, this is known locally as Boots folly, stories abound as to why Charles Boot had the tower built in 1926/7, one being that it was constructed to find work for his stone masons in those lean times. Charles Boot at this time lived at the previously mentioned Moscar Lodge.

18

Stanage Pole.

Stanage Edge - view towards High Neb.

The Dyke Dale Disaster
2 miles to Strines Inn.

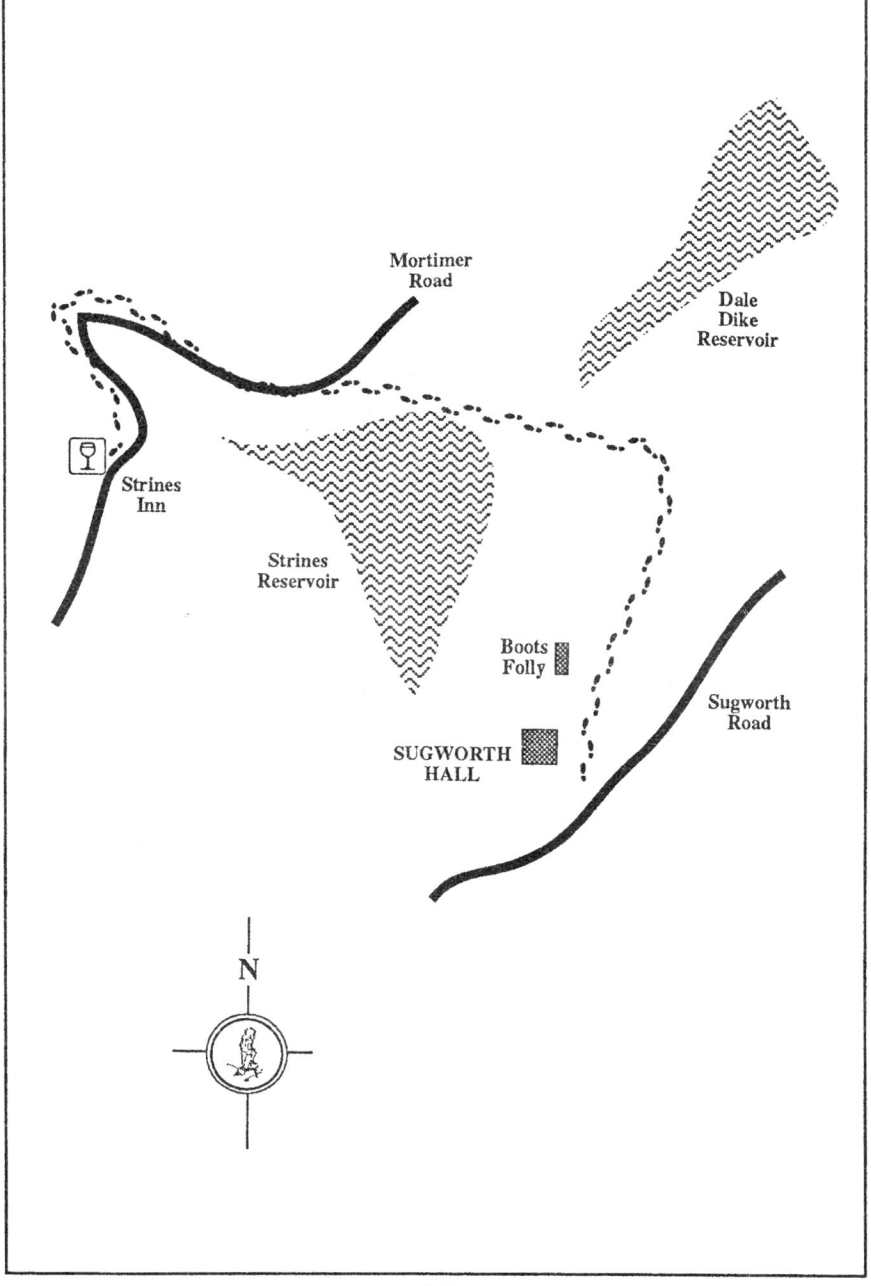

Mortimer Road

Dale Dike Reservoir

Strines Inn

Strines Reservoir

Boots Folly

SUGWORTH HALL

Sugworth Road

N

THE DYKE DALE DISASTER
- 2 miles to Strines Inn

Map - 1:25,000 Pathfinder Series Sheet No. SK29/39 - Sheffield (North) and Stocksbridge.

Standing by Boots Folly you have a magnificent view down the Bradfield Dale, the lower of the two dams at this location is the ill fated Dale Dyke dam.

The dam had just been completed in 1864 and had been filled to its 700 million gallons capacity, when just before midnight on March 11th 1864, a very stormy windy night, the dam wall which was ninety five feet high and four hundred and eighteen feet long started to collapse under the strain. After a while the wall was breached and a wall of water started to thunder down the valley towards an unsuspecting and sleeping population. The ensuing flood destroyed everything in its path and caused considerable loss of life. Altogether almost two hundred and fifty people died on that fateful night. After the tragedy the dam was rebuilt four hundred yards further up the valley. At the time of this tragic event my great grandfather William Hiley was a Police Sergeant in Sheffield and I am sure he and his Colleagues must have had a busy night.

Follow the path downhill, you come to a stile over the stone wall near the base of the Strines dam, climb over and go to your left, go over the left hand footbridge and take the path up to the house by the side of the dam. From here continue up the track to the road and turn left, the last mile is a bit of an uphill slog but a well earned pint at the Strines Inn is a just reward at the end of a good days walk.

View to Dale Dyke Dam.

Boots Folly.

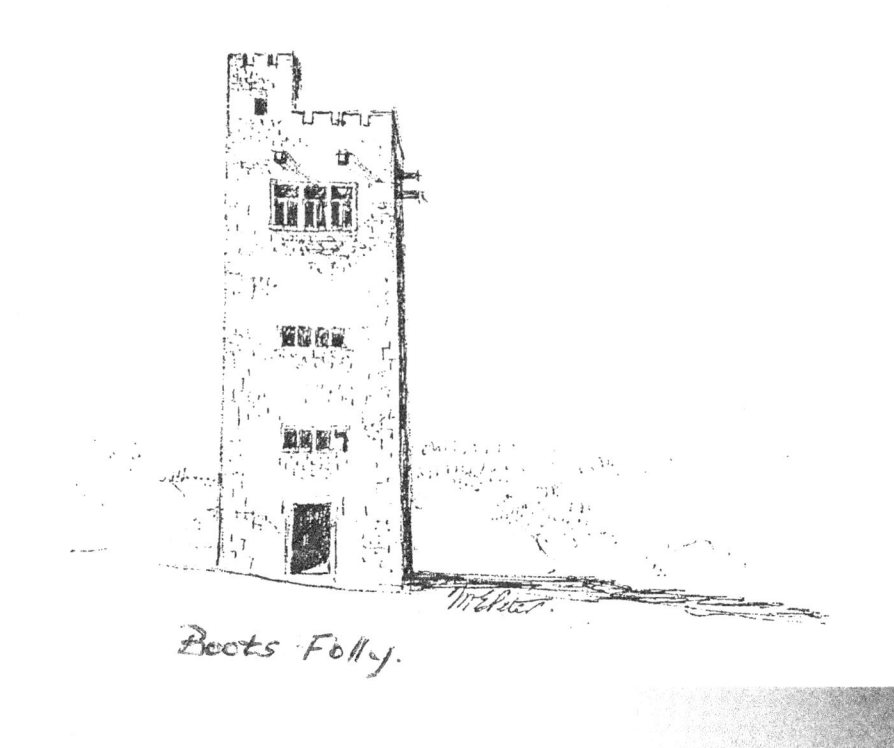

Strines Dam from Boots Folly. Strines Inn in the distance.

STRINES INN

The Strines In started life in 1275 as a farm and manor house. During the sixteenth century it belonged to the Worrall family and still bears the family Coat of Arms above the door.

Although in an isolated place it is a very popular pub, well known for its excellent food, and bed and breakfast is available, however, advanced booking is advisable especially at weekends. Having arrived, had your evening meal and a couple of pints Beware as you retire to your cozy room sleep with one eye open, you never know you may see the grey lady who it is said haunts this ancient Inn.

Strines Inn.

Strines to Derwent Valley - 7 miles

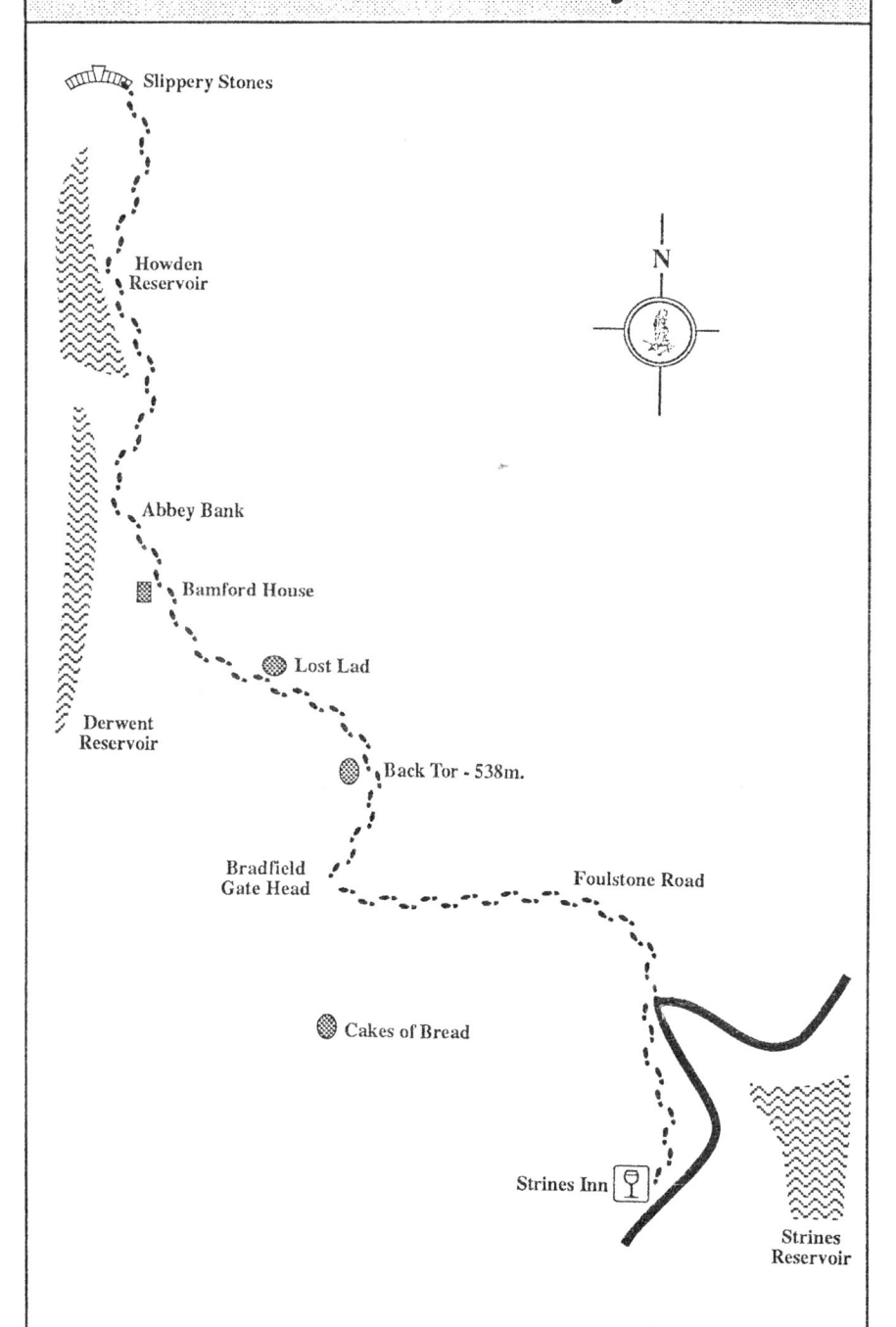

Slippery Stones

Howden Reservoir

N

Abbey Bank

Bamford House

Lost Lad

Derwent Reservoir

Back Tor - 538m.

Bradfield Gate Head

Foulstone Road

Cakes of Bread

Strines Inn

Strines Reservoir

24

STRINES TO DERWENT VALLEY
- 7 miles

Maps - 1:25,000 Pathfinder Series Sheet No. SK29/39 - Sheffield (North) and Stocksbridge.
1:25,000 Outdoor Leisure map - The Dark Peak.

Leaving the Strines Inn, turn left down the lane. Just past the cottage on your right by the side of the wall you will see an old stone. On the stone are the words "Take Off". This stone marks the spot where in the old days the horses would have been unharnessed and rested after pulling their loads up the steep hill.

Continue down the hill and over the bridge at the bottom. Before the bridge was built there used to be stepping stones across the river at this point. Just over the bridge turn left and through the car park, at the top follow the track up to a gate. Continue over the stile and follow the path all the way up to Bradfield Gates. The moor you are now crossing along with many more in the Peak District is kept for grouse shooting, the shooting butts can be seen on either side of the path.

The call of these birds along with the curlew are a welcome sound on a summers day. This area along with other parts of the Peak Park is also home to the rare mountain hare. If seen in summer all brown but in winter changes the colour of his coat to a whitish grey. As you reach the top of the path you arrive at the Derwent edge at Bradfield Gates. Standing at this point with your back to where you have just walked you see in the distance before you the Derwent Valley. Away to your front on a good day you can see all the way to Bleaklow and Kinder Scout. To your left stretches Derwent Edge with its rock formations with such names as "Cakes of Bread" and Salt Cellar". I often wonder what long forgotten soul gave them these names.

Leaving Bradfield Gates turn right and head for the triangulation point at Back Tor. As you walk along this path you can see much work has been done to combat the erosion of this fragile landscape. We should congratulate the rangers and volunteers who carry out this heavy back breaking work for our benefit.

As you approach the rocks at Back Tor follow the now flagstoned path to your left. I now call this stretch of the path the yellow brick road, but I must say it is far better than being up to your ankles in mud. Follow this path to the cairn at Lost Lad. The cairn marks the spot where many years ago the body of a lost shepherd boy was found. He had gone up onto the moors from the old Derwent village to gather the family sheep, when he was lost in a blizzard. Before he died he managed to scratch on a stone the words, Lost Lad. The cairn now marks his last resting place. Nowadays whenever local shepherds pass this spot they place a stone on the cairn as a mark of respect for their forebear. Leaving Lost Lad follow the path down and across the open moor below, as you walk for a change on flat ground and the legs are not working so hard pause for a moment and look at your lovely surroundings, its hard to believe how harsh and deadly this place can be in winter. Take the case of a Mr. J. Tagg, he was a retired shepherd who lived in the Derwent Valley. In December 1953 he went up onto the moors with his dog Tip, again the weather closed in and he got lost and died. His body was not found until March 1954, Tip had stayed with his dead master all this time and although very close to death he was still alive. He lived for another year after being found. A Memorial to his heroic dog stands beside the Derwent dam not far from the West Tower. Truly a man could never have a greater friend. His faithful dog had stayed with him for fifteen weeks.

As you walk along the track look down the valley to your left, you can on a good day see all the way down to the Ladybower dam and the viaduct which carries the A57 Snake road across that part of it. Continue along the track until you come to a fork, take the right hand path and over the stile at the fence. Turn right and follow the path down to a signpost where two paths cross, take the path to the right for Howden dam and Abbey brook. You are now in the Derwent valley, to my mind the most beautiful area in the whole of the Peak District. The valley of course is dominated by the magnificent structures of the Derwent and Howden dams. The building of these dams must be one of the major engineering feats of the early part of this century. Work started on the dams in 1901 and the valley was a hive of industry for the next fifteen years until the completion of the project.

During the construction of the dams an entire village was built for the workforce, it was complete with its own Hospital, Police Station, School, Pub, and even allotments for the workers to grow their own produce. Alas nothing of the village remains today, however there are reminders of the railway which brought all the stone from the quarries near Grindleford. The Derwent dam has been made famous for the part it played along with other stretches of water for practice runs by the famous Dam Busters 617 Sqdn. R.A.F. A stone to mark these events is located in the west tower. There have been some very good books written about the Derwent valley and the construction of the dams. Ones that spring to mind are *Silent Valley* by Vic Hallam and *Walls Across The Valley* by Brian Robinson.

However back to your walk, as you walk along the path towards Howden the views of the valley below on a good day are some of the best you will see anywhere. As you walk along turn and look at the wonderful view behind the imposing wall and towers of the Derwent dam. After a while you lose sight of this dam but almost at once you are confronted by the twin towers of the Howden dam. On reaching the track which runs around the dams turn right and follow it until you reach the old packhorse bridge at Slippery Stones. The bridge used to span the river Derwent much lower down stream in the now sunken village of Derwent. It stood opposite the old Derwent Hall. When the village was to be flooded the bridge was taken down and re-erected at its present location at a later date. Thank heaven someone had the foresight to salvage something from that once proud village. A mile or so above the bridge is the source of the river Derwent, being the longest river in Derbyshire, it flows for some sixty miles before joining the river Trent. As it snakes through the countryside it passes through such lovely places as Chatsworth and Matlock.

Howden Dam.

Derwent to Flouch - 6 miles

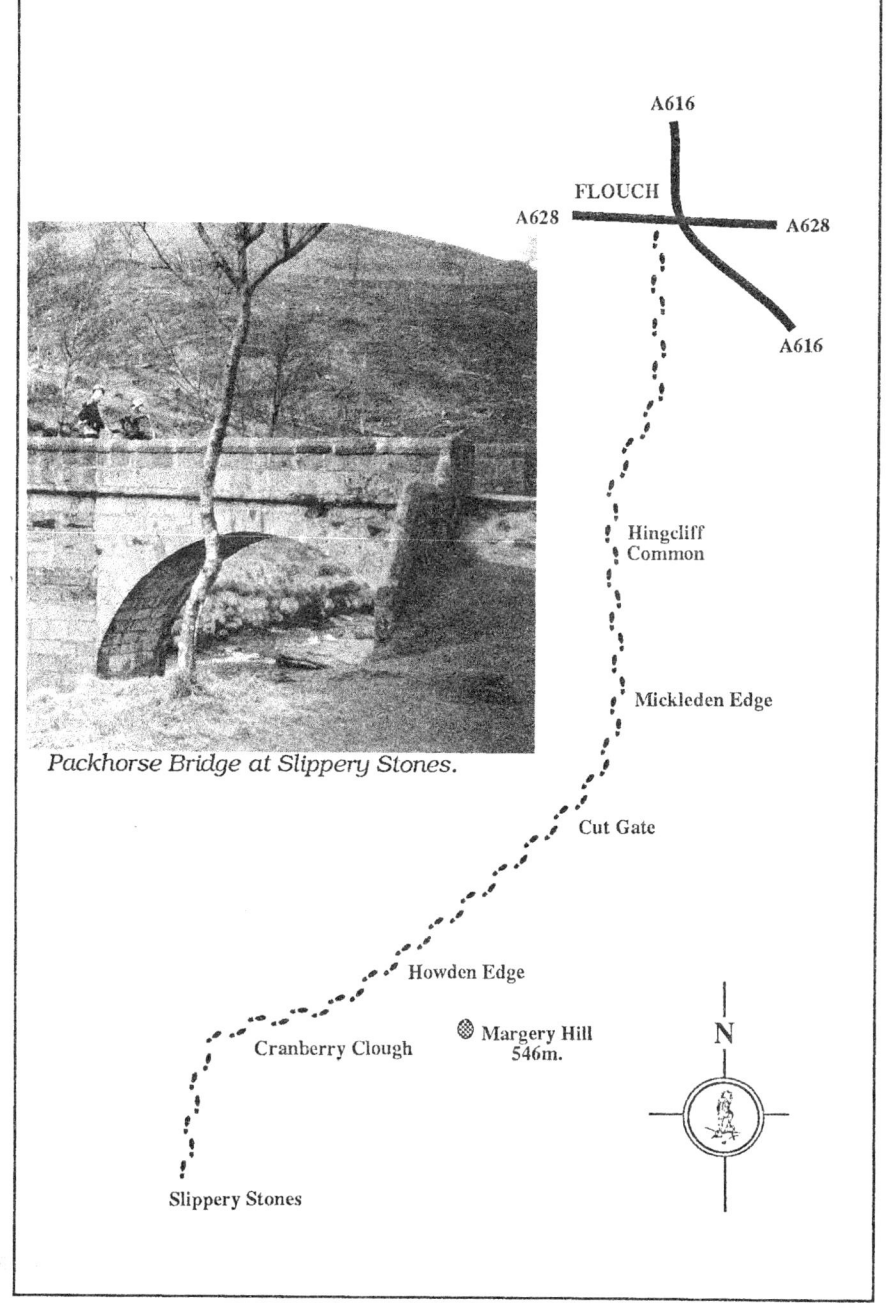

Packhorse Bridge at Slippery Stones.

A616
FLOUCH
A628
A628
A616

Hingcliff Common

Mickleden Edge

Cut Gate

Howden Edge

Cranberry Clough

⊛ Margery Hill
546m.

Slippery Stones

N

28

DERWENT TO FLOUCH - 6 miles

Map - 1:25,000 OutdoorLeisure Map - The Dark Paek.
Leaving Slippery Stones do not go over the bridge but take the path past the sheepfold. The path takes you to the bottom of Cranberry Clough, after crossing the footbridge the path forks. Take the path to your right marked by a blue arrow. You are now walking on the old packhorse track called Cut Gate. It takes you out of the Derwent valley and over the moors via Howden Edge to the Flouch Inn. As you start to climb from the bottom of the clough the way has been made a lot easier again by our intrepid volunteers. The Cut Gate track was used by the farmers of the woodlands valley as the Derwent valley used to be called. They used it to take their produce to the market at Penistone. Its hard to believe now what a busy thoroughfare it must have been with packhorses and people on market days in those far off times. The track used to be maintained and financed jointly by the farmers and the Duke of Rutland, he used to reside at the Derwent Hall. As you climb out of Cranberry Clough and across the open moors towards Howden Edge think of the pack animals who did this and other such journeys in all weathers. Time and time again carrying their heavy loads, where would we be now if we had not been given that noble creature the horse.

As you reach the summit at Howden Edge on a clear day in the distance can be seen two modern day landmarks. Looking over o your left is the television mast at Holme Moss which stands at 750 feet, and looking straight forward is the even taller mast at Emley Moor. Standing at 1000 feet it is the tallest structure in Europe. Continue along the path until on your right there is a path sign posted to Langsett and Penistone. Do not turn here but carry on forward to the bridge at the head of the Langsett Reservoir. Crossing over the bridge, follow the track marked by the blue arrows until you come to a sign post for the Flouch Inn and Hazelhead Station. Turn left and follow the path until you reach the A628 road, this is the very busy trunk road which takes the heavy goods traffic across the Pennines via the Woodhead Pass. The section of road here is new and has replaced the old Flouch cross roads with a new roundabout. Cross over the road and follow the path to the old road. It is hard to believe seeing it now just how busy this road used to be. Down to your right is the Flouch Inn, the present building is the second to have the name, the original inn is opposite and is now a lovely cottage. The present inn is now a Chinese restaurant, a shame really. I am more for a pint and a port pie. Walk up the road from the Flouch and take the path on your right beside the white cottages.

Flouch to Hepworth -7 miles

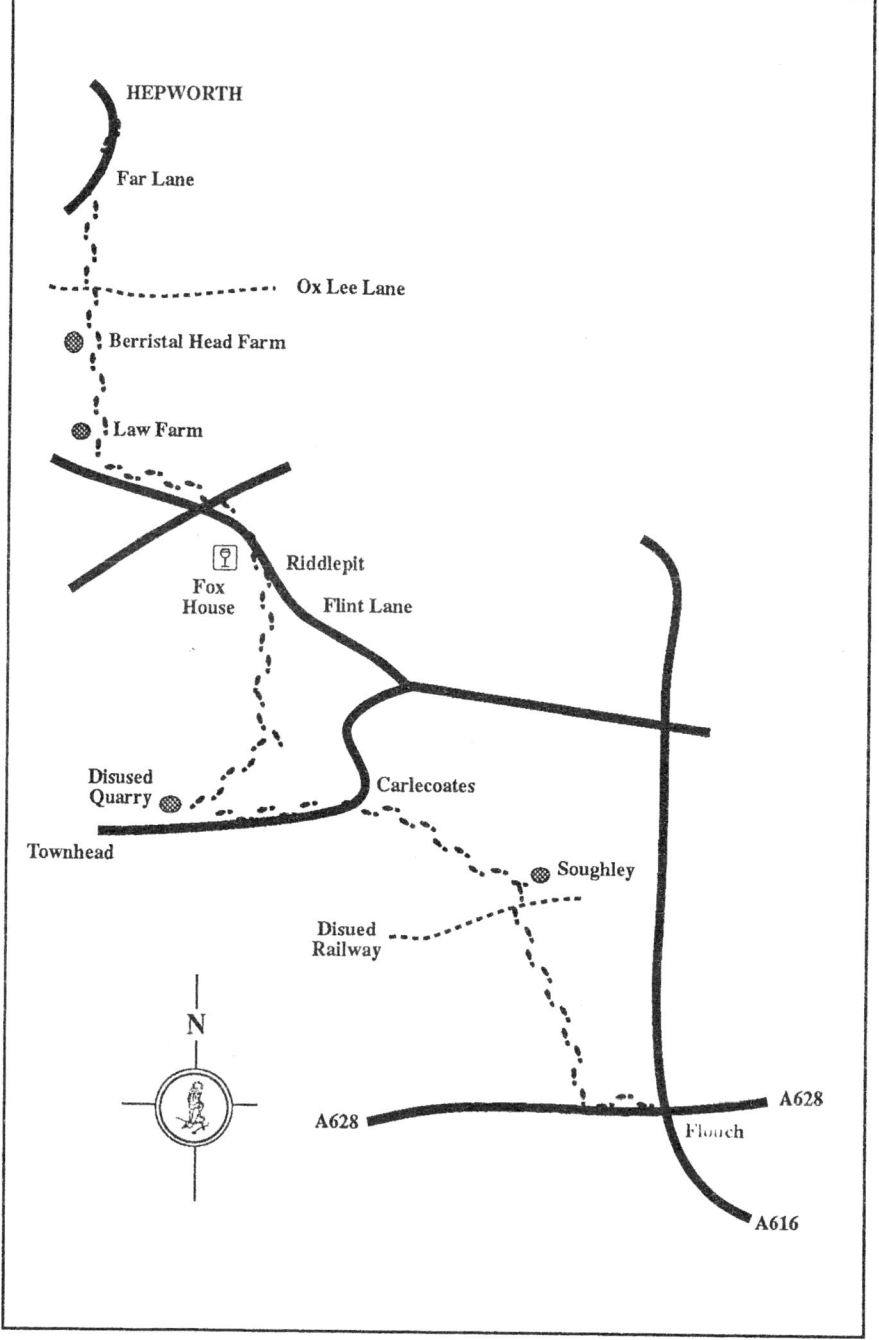

FLOUCH TO HEPWORTH
- 7 miles

Map - 1:25,000 Pathfinder Series Sheet No. SE00/10 - Holmfirth and Saddleworth Moor.

Follow this path until you reach the old disused railway track, this is the track that linked Sheffield to Manchester. Two miles or so along the track to the west are the Woodhead tunnels. The three tunnels were built at a very high cost in human life, the first one being completed in 1845 with twenty six workmen having lost their lives. With the demise of the railway the tunnels are now used to carry high voltage cables across the Pennines.

Leaving the bridge you descend down to the footbridge which spans the river Don. The Don has its source not far away up on the high moors, the first service it does for man is to fill the large Winscar reservoir. From our present location it meanders through the woods and valleys until it reaches Sheffield where for many years it has been the life blood of that cities industry. Providing the world with the finest steel and cutlery money can buy. Today the Don is no longer the polluted river she once was, now there are fish in her waters and walks along the banks, who knows one day we may even have salmon back at Salmon Pastures.

After crossing the bridge carry on up the path to Soughley, here the most imposing building to me is the huge cathedral like barn. At the lane in front of the farm turn left then right through the gate, follow the path waymarked by white arrows up across the fields to the hamlet of Carlecoates. As you arrive at this ancient little place you pass the lovely old church of St. Anne's, just past the church at the lane an old barn bears the date 1662. Carlcoates being 1000 feet above sea level has some excellent views of the surrounding countryside. Turn left along the lane and you pass on your right the old village school house, now turned into a very nice bungalow. Continue along the lane for about half a mile then take the path on your right beside the old quarry. Follow the path to the road at Riddlepit. You have now entered Summer Wine Country. The farm on your left is the location used as the home of the one and only Seymour Utterthwait. It is sad to think that Michael Aldridge is no longer with us, I can still see his beaming smile when he knew he had conned Compo and Cleggy into some scheme or other. Turning left up the lane you come to the Fox House Inn, a favoured watering hole for the dynamic trio, remember the time they along with Captain Zero were thrown out of this pub for standing on the tables, and Ely cleared it of all customers when he decided to play darts. There must be many a landlord wishes he could clear his pub as fast at closing time.

Continue along the road to the cross roads, go straight ahead and after a few yards you cross over into West Yorkshire. This is the third county you have walked in on your journey, and just as South Yorkshire was built on steel West Yorkshire was built on textiles, but more of this later. As you walk along the road to your front in the distance is another modern day landmark, this is the huge wind generator at Longley Farm, it stands at 70 feet tall and generates power for the dairy. The dairy which in my opinion makes the best yogurt around. About a half mile passed the cross roads take the path on your right at Law Farm, the path starts at a stile over the garden wall beside the fire hydrant. The path is waymarked by yellow arrows and takes you down past Berristal Head Farm, as you walk along these out of the way places keep a sharp lookout, you never know who might be lurking in the bushes, you could stumble across Howard and Marina.

After passing Berristal Head Farm go over the stile onto the track at Ox Lee Lane, cross over the track and follow the path down to the road. Turn right here and follow the road down into the village of Hepworth, as you walk along you feel as though at any time you could be confronted by Foggy and Cleggy followed by a scruffy little man in wellies lagging behind and complaining that the hills are getting steeper, and do you know what, I think be could be right.

Carlecoats.

Hepworth Church.

Horse Troughs, Hepworth.

Hepworth to Holmfirth - 3 1/2 miles

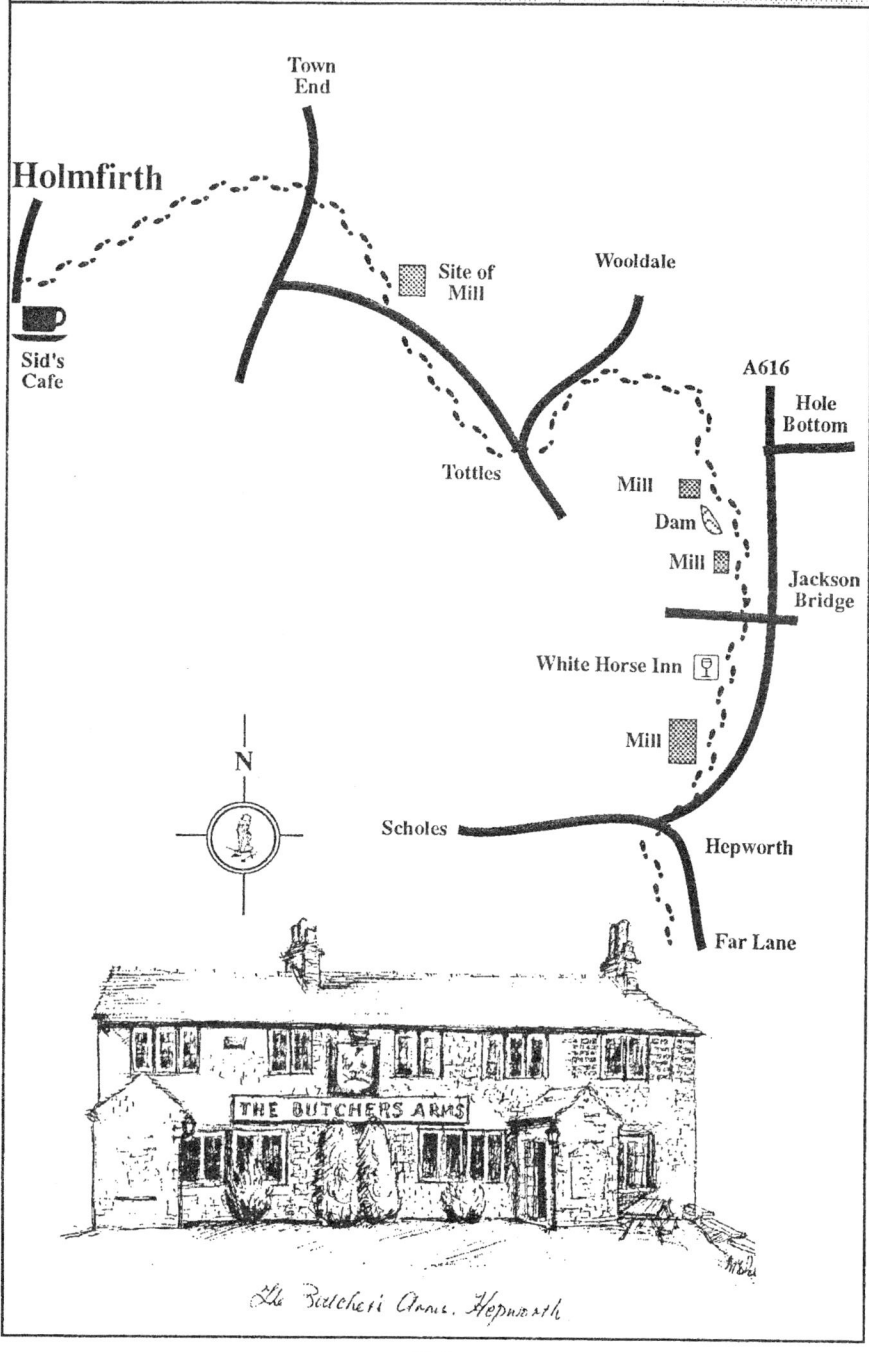

Holmfirth
Sid's Cafe
Town End
Site of Mill
Wooldale
A616
Hole Bottom
Tottles
Mill
Dam
Mill
Jackson Bridge
White Horse Inn
Mill
Scholes
Hepworth
Far Lane

N

The Butchers Arms, Hepworth

HEPWORTH TO HOLMFIRTH - 3 1/2 miles

Map - 1:25,000 Pathfinder Series Sheet No. SE 00/10 - Holmfirth and Saddleworth Moor.

The village of Hepworth dates back all the way to the Doomsday Book, with its stone built cottages it gives you the feeling it will last forever. Many of the old weavers cottages you see date back to the 17th century, before the days of the mills and factories. Indeed the back bone of the textile industry used to be the hundreds of such cottages and farms spread throughout the counties of Yorkshire and Lancashire. Then with the coming of the water wheel and later steam engines the industry started to go through a dramatic change. The source of power was now in the valley bottoms, and the mills that were built along with the housing for the workers created the many towns and villages we see today. As you walk through Hepworth again we find a location used in Summer Wine, this is the Butchers Arms. Accommodation is available here if you require it at this stage of your walk. Leaving the pub walk down the road towards the church, turn right down Dean Bridge Lane, this takes you to the church gates. Take the path to your left and follow it to the John Woodhead (Dobroyd Mill). John Woodhead like many of the old mill owners was a local man from Holmfirth. He started trading in 1862 by making yarn for the local weaving industry, delivering it by horse and cart. His original mill was built at Thongsbridge four miles from the present site. It was by the river and powered by water then steam. The company has now traded for 120 years. Walk beside the mill and at the bottom of the car park you find the mill shop, a good place to pick up a bargain or two. around the side of the shop the path takes you down to the road, turn left and walk down to Jackson Bridge. At this point you get a better view of the old mill, a lot of it is now used for light industry. The White Horse Inn is again a favoured drinking place for Compo and company. Remember the time he disappeared over the wall here when having his picture taken in his uniform posing with Wesley's motorbike. Again if required accommodation is available at the pub. Just up the hill from here at the village of Scholes was born that much loved entertainer Roy Castle. Before carrying on if you look up behind the pub the row of cottages on the hillside are the homes of Cleggy, Howard and Pearl. Leaving Jackson Bridge continue up the road towards Mear House keeping the river on your left you come to a row of cottages called Mear House Terrace, one of these is a very nice guest house, Fair View. At the end of the cottages on your left turn down the steps which will take you down to the old Shaley Mill. Like many more the mill has closed, but this one has a new lease of life having been converted into a very nice housing scheme. As you walk through the car parking area keep the river on your left and take the path at the end of the car park into the woods beside the river. Follow this path until you reach yet another mill. This is the Wildstar Mill, again it is almost 100 years old. This mill is where textiles are dyed. The path at this point follows the side of the building under the prefabricated office. Around the side of the mill keep to the right of the round black tank and follow the path up to the road.

At the road turn left up the hill to the lovely hamlet of Totties. Again this place abounds with old weavers cottages, a place where time has stood still, I am sure if you close your eyes and listen you can still hear the sound of the looms working away in the upstairs rooms. At the road junction turn right and follow the lane until you come to the site of yet another old mill. This one however has been demolished and in its place is a new housing complex called Fearnly Court, the houses having been built in the old cottage style with stone mullioned windows. Just along the road you come to a track at two old stone gate posts beside a small bungalow, turn right here and follow the track to a gate. Go through the gate and follow the path up to the road at Town End. Town End is a very interesting place with its old pub, chapel and of course the local Co-op Store. A cottage beside the Co-op has a date stone for 1621. On reaching the road on the opposite side you take the path marked by a yellow arrow, the marker is actually on the telegraph pole, the path takes you up South Street past the old cottages. As you leave the village behind, walk along the path until you come to a stile opposite a gate, again you have the yellow way marker, go over the stile and follow the path until you emerge from between the stone walls and are met by the most wonderful view of Holme Valley. Cross the track in front of you and take the path downhill passed the back of the cottages onto the road. At the road turn left and walk along until you reach the second turning on your right, turn right here, the building on your right at this location is the old Cliff school house which was one of the oldest schools in Holmfirth. From here just keep walking downhill towards the church tower and you will arrive in the square beside the church and Sid's cafe. You have arrived at Holmfirth the heart of Summer Wine country, although much of the towns prosperity comes from the tourists thanks to that wonderful T.V series with its gentle humour and magnificent scenery, these are the modern day trappings. We must not forget the town was born out of the industrialrevolution and all the hardship this implied. The church and most of the older buildings date back to the 18th century. As you walk around the town and take in the sites, you will find in Towngate the old Genn Monument. It stands on the site of the old village stocks, it bears a plate marking the height of the great flood. Over the years Holmfirth has been subjected to four floods, but by far the worst was in 1852. On February 5th of that year the Bilberry reservoir burst its banks and the waters thundered down the valley into the town. A total of 81 lives were lost on that fateful night, the dam was rebuilt and now along with the larger Dingley reservoir is a local beauty spot.

Well having now completed your walk from Hunters Bar to Summer Wine, and I hope you had a cuppa in Sids Cafe', take a good look around the area and soak up its gentle atmosphere before you go on your way.

This walk is dedicated to the memory of Michael Bates, Joe Gladwin, John Comer and Michael Aldridge sadly no longer with us.

White Horse, Jackson Bridge. Howard and Cleggs coattages are up behind the pub.

37

LOG

DATE STARTED..

DATE COMPLETED..

ROUTE POINT	MILE NO.	ARR.	DEP.	COMMENTS WEATHER
Hunter's Bar	-			
Forge	2			
Porter Brook	4			
Knoll Top Farm	6			
Redmires Dams	8			
Stanage Edge	10			
Boots Folly	14 1/2			
Strines Inn	16 1/2			
Back Tor	20			
Slippery Stones	23 1/2			
Cut Gate	25			
Flouch	29 1/2			
Riddlepit	32			
Hepworth	36			
Holmfirth	39			

Compo's Way

Badges measure 3 1/2" wide by 3" high and are yellow cloth with brown, black, red and white embroidery.

BADGE ORDER FORM

Date completed ....

Time ....

Name..

Address ....

....

Price - £3.00 each including postage, VAT and signed certificate.

"I've done a John Merrill Walk" T shirt - Emerald Green with white lettering - all sizes - £7.50 including postage and VAT.

JOHN MERRILL'S HAPPY WALKING CAP - £3.00

From - El Morro Equipment Ltd., 19, Moseley Street, Ripley, Derbyshire. DE5 3DA

☎ 01773 - 512143

.... You may photocopy this form if needed ....

THE JOHN MERRILL CHALLENGE WALK BADGE - walk this route twice or complete another of John Merrill's Challenge Walks and send details and cheque for £3.00 for a special 2 challenge walk circular four colour embroidered badge,

Amenities Guide -

I have listed some places for accommodation along the route.

🍴🛏🍷 The Strines Inn, Strines Nr. Sheffield. Phone No. 0114 - 2851247
The Butchers Arms, Hepworth, Nr. Holmfirth. Phone No. 01484 - 682857
White Horse Inn, Jackson Bridge. Phone No. 01484 - 683940
Fair View Guest House, Jackson Bridge, Phone No. 01484 - 681643
Langsett Youth Hostel, Langsett, Nr Sheffield. Phone No. 0114 - 2884541
The Wagon and Horses, Langsett, Nr Sheffield. Phone No. 01226 - 763147

ℹ️ In Holmfirth there is a very good Tourist Information Centre Phone No. 01484- 687603.

Old Barnside House,
5, Barnside Lane, Hepworth, Holmfirth.
Contact: Anne Senior
6, Barnside Lane, Hepworth, Holmfirth, HD7 1TN
Tel. 01484 - 686610

🔑🔑🔑 COMMENDED

Beautiful stone-built 17th century cottage, in heart of Summer Wine Country yet close to Peak National Park. Situated in the peaceful rural hamlet of Barnside. Very comfortably furnished and equipped with double and twin rooms, c/h, colour TV's, washer etc. Gas Central Heating and all linen included in price.
Special weekend and midweek rates - October - April. Brochure.
£135 - £225 per week. Sleeps 5 + cot.

Corn Loft House,
146, Woodhead Road, Holmbridge, Holmfirth. HD7 1NL
Tel. 01484 - 683147

Bed & Breakfast from £17 with en suite rooms. Trevor and Kath give a warm welcome to walkers in the Summer Wine/Peak District country.

Attention Walkers!

Why not have a good, hearty breakfast
at the end or beginning of
the Compo Way
after spending a restful night
at

Hunter House Hotel,

Hunters Bar,
Sheffield.
South Yorkshire
S11 8TG
Tel. 0114 266 2709
Fax. 0114 268 6370

SPECIAL RATES Bed & Breakfast -
* £23 p.p. sharing, en-suite.
* £20 p.p. sharing, standard.
* £24 p.p. single, standard.

SUMMER WINE COTTAGES

West Royd Farm, Marsh Lane, Shepley, Huddersfield. HD8 8AY
Contact: Mrs. M. Brook. Tel. 01484 - 602147

Part of a beautifully converted 17th century farmhouse in six acres of Pennine farmland close to Summer Wine country.
Linen, towels, c/h and power inclusive. Pets by arrangement only. Owners' heated swimming pool for hire. Stabling available - horse £25 a week.
<u>Granary Cottage</u> - 1 double, shower room, open plan kitchen/lounge with sofa bed, colour TV and video.
<u>Harvest Cottage</u> - 1 double bedroom, I bedroom with bunkbeds, shower room, sopen plan kitchen-dining area, lounge, colour TV, video and washer dryer.
£100.00 - £200.00   Sleeps 2 and 4.

"From footprint to finished book."

OTHER BOOKS by FOOTPRINT PRESS LTD.,

CIRCULAR WALK GUIDES -
SHORT CIRCULAR WALKS IN THE PEAK DISTRICT - Vol. 1,2 and 3
CIRCULAR WALKS IN WESTERN PEAKLAND
SHORT CIRCULAR WALKS IN THE STAFFORDSHIRE MOORLANDS
SHORT CIRCULAR WALKS - TOWNS & VILLAGES OF THE PEAK DISTRICT
SHORT CIRCULAR WALKS AROUND MATLOCK
SHORT CIRCULAR WALKS IN THE DUKERIES
SHORT CIRCULAR WALKS IN SOUTH YORKSHIRE
SHORT CIRCULAR WALKS IN SOUTH DERBYSHIRE
SHORT CIRCULAR WALKS AROUND BUXTON
SHORT CIRCULAR WALKS AROUND WIRKSWORTH
SHORT CIRCULAR WALKS IN THE HOPE VALLEY
40 SHORT CIRCULAR WALKS IN THE PEAK DISTRICT
CIRCULAR WALKS ON KINDER & BLEAKLOW
SHORT CIRCULAR WALKS IN SOUTH NOTTINGHAMSHIRE
SHIRT CIRCULAR WALKS IN CHESHIRE
SHORT CIRCULAR WALKS IN WEST YORKSHIRE
CIRCULAR WALKS TO PEAK DISTRICT AIRCRAFT WRECKS by John Mason
CIRCULAR WALKS IN THE DERBYSHIRE DALES
SHORT CIRCULAR WALKS IN EAST DEVON
SHORT CIRCULAR WALKS AROUND HARROGATE
SHORT CIRCULAR WALKS IN CHARNWOOD FOREST
SHORT CIRCULAR WALKS AROUND CHESTERFIELD
SHORT CIRCULAR WALKS IN THE YORKS DALES - Vol 1 - Southern area.
SHORT CIRCULAR WALKS IN THE AMBER VALLEY (Derbyshire)
SHORT CIRCULAR WALKS IN THE LAKE DISTRICT
SHORT CIRCULAR WALKS IN THE NORTH YORKSHIRE MOORS
SHORT CIRCULAR WALKS IN EAST STAFFORDSHIRE
DRIVING TO WALK - 16 Short Circular walks south of London by Dr. Simon Archer Vol 1 and 2
LONG CIRCULAR WALKS IN THE PEAK DISTRICT - Vol.1,2 and 3.
LONG CIRCULAR WALKS IN THE STAFFORDSHIRE MOORLANDS
LONG CIRCULAR WALKS IN CHESHIRE
WALKING THE TISSINGTON TRAIL
WALKING THE HIGH PEAK TRAIL
WALKING THE MONSAL TRAIL & OTHER DERBYSHIRE TRAILS

CANAL WALKS -
VOL 1 - DERBYSHIRE & NOTTINGHAMSHIRE
VOL 2 - CHESHIRE & STAFFORDSHIRE
VOL 3 - STAFFORDSHIRE
VOL 4 - THE CHESHIRE RING
VOL 5 - LINCOLNSHIRE & NOTTINGHAMSHIRE
VOL 6 - SOUTH YORKSHIRE
VOL 7 - THE TRENT & MERSEY CANAL
VOL 8 - WALKING THE DERBY CANAL RING

JOHN MERRILL DAY CHALLENGE WALKS -
WHITE PEAK CHALLENGE WALK
DARK PEAK CHALLENGE WALK
PEAK DISTRICT END TO END WALKS
STAFFORDSHIRE MOORLANDS CHALLENGE WALK

THE LITTLE JOHN CHALLENGE WALK
NORTH YORKSHIRE MOORS CHALLENGE WALK
LAKELAND CHALLENGE WALK
THE RUTLAND WATER CHALLENGE WALK
MALVERN HILLS CHALLENGE WALK
THE SALTER'S WAY
THE SNOWDON CHALLENGE
CHARNWOOD FOREST CHALLENGE WALK
THREE COUNTIES CHALLENGE WALK (Peak District).
CAL-DER-WENT WALK by Geoffrey Carr,
THE QUANTOCK WAY
BELVOIR WITCHES CHALLENGE WALK

YORKSHIRE DALES CHALLENGE WALK

THE CARNEDDAU CHALLENGE WALK

INSTRUCTION & RECORD -
HIKE TO BE FIT.....STROLLING WITH JOHN
THE JOHN MERRILL WALK RECORD BOOK

MULTIPLE DAY WALKS -
THE RIVERS'S WAY
PEAK DISTRICT: HIGH LEVEL ROUTE
PEAK DISTRICT MARATHONS
THE LIMEY WAY
THE PEAKLAND WAY

COAST WALKS & NATIONAL TRAILS -
ISLE OF WIGHT COAST PATH
PEMBROKESHIRE COAST PATH
THE CLEVELAND WAY
WALKING ANGELSEY'S COASTLINE.

CYCLING Compiled by Arnold Robinson.
CYCLING AROUND THE NORTH YORK MOORS .   CYCLING AROUND MATLOCK. LEICES & RUTLAND.
CYCLING AROUND CASTLETON & the Hope Valley. CYCLING AROUND CHESTERFIELD.
CYCLING IN THE YORKSHIRE WOLDS   CYCLING AROUND BUXTON. LINCOLNSHIRE.

PEAK DISTRICT HISTORICAL GUIDES -
A to Z GUIDE OF THE PEAK DISTRICT
DERBYSHIRE INNS - an A to Z guide
HALLS AND CASTLES OF THE PEAK DISTRICT & DERBYSHIRE
TOURING THE PEAK DISTRICT & DERBYSHIRE BY CAR
DERBYSHIRE FOLKLORE
PUNISHMENT IN DERBYSHIRE
CUSTOMS OF THE PEAK DISTRICT & DERBYSHIRE
WINSTER - a souvenir guide
ARKWRIGHT OF CROMFORD
LEGENDS OF DERBYSHIRE
DERBYSHIRE FACTS & RECORDS
TALES FROM THE MINES by Geoffrey Carr
PEAK DISTRICT PLACE NAMES by Martin Spray

JOHN MERRILL'S MAJOR WALKS -
TURN RIGHT AT LAND'S END
WITH MUSTARD ON MY BACK
TURN RIGHT AT DEATH VALLEY
EMERALD COAST WALK

SKETCH BOOKS -
SKETCHES OF THE PEAK DISTRICT

COLOUR BOOK:-
THE PEAK DISTRICT.......something to remember her by.

For a free catalogue of all the books write to -
Footprint Press Ltd.,
19, Moseley Street,
Ripley,
Derbyshire.
DE5 3DA

OVERSEAS GUIDES -
HIKING IN NEW MEXICO - Vol I - The Sandia and Manzano Mountains.
Vol 2 - Hiking "Billy the Kid" Country. Vol 4 - N.W. area - " Hiking Indian Country."
"WALKING IN DRACULA COUNTRY" - Romania.

VISITOR GUIDES - MATLOCK . BAKEWELL. ASHBOURNE.

OTHER CHALLENGE WALKS BY JOHN N. MERRILL

DAY CHALLENGES -

John Merrill's White Peak Challenge Walk - 25 miles.
Circular walk from Bakewell involving 3,600 feet of ascent.

John Merrill's Dark Peak Challenge Walk - 24 miles.
Circular walk from Hathersage involving 3,300 feet of ascent.

John Merrill's Staffordshire Moorlands Challenge Walk - 26 miles. Circular walk from Oakamoor involving 2,200 feet of ascent.

John Merrill's Yorkshire Dales Challenge Walk - 23 miles.
Circular walk from Kettlewell involving 3,600 feet of ascent.

John Merrill's North Yorkshire Moors Challenge Walk - 24 miles.
Circular walk from Goathland - a seaside bash - involving 2,000 feet of ascent.

The Little John Challenge Walk - 28 miles.
Circular walk from Edwinstowe in Sherwood Forest - Robin Hood country.

Peak District End to End Walks.
1. Gritstone Edge Walk - 23 miles down the eastern edge system.
2. Limestone Dale Walk - 24 miles down the limestone dales from Buxton to Ashbourne.

The Rutland Water Challenge walk - 24 miles
Around the shore of Rutland Water, the largest man made reservoir in Britain.

The Malvern Hills Challenge Walk - 20 miles.
Beneath and along the crest of the Malvern Hills.

The Salter's Way - 25 miles.
Across Cheshire from Northwich to the Pennines, following an old salt way.

John Merrill's Snowdon Challenge Walk - 30 miles.
A tough day walk involving 5,000 feet of ascent and descent from the sea to the summit of Snowdon AND BACK!

John Merrill's Three Counties Challenge Walk - 28 miles.
A tough walk from Tittesworth Reservoir over the Roaches, Shutlingsloe, Shining Tor and Flash - in Staffordshire, Cheshire and Derbyshire.